Contents

Words that appear in the glossary are printed in **bold** the first time
they occur in the text.

Exploring our environment

Look around you. You see forests, fields, lakes and rivers. You see farms, factories, houses and cities. All these things make up our **environment**. Sometimes there are problems with the environment. For instance in many places the air we breathe is polluted. It often looks dirty and sometimes even smells. Why is the air dirty? How does dirty air harm us and other living things? Let's find out.

4

ASK ISAAC ASIMOV ?

Why is the air dirty?

Heinemann

First published in Great Britain by Heinemann Library
an imprint of Heinemann Publishers (Oxford) Ltd
Halley Court, Jordan Hill, Oxford OX2 8EJ

OXFORD LONDON EDINBURGH MADRID
ATHENS BOLOGNA PARIS MELBOURNE
SYDNEY AUCKLAND SINGAPORE TOKYO
IBADAN NAIROBI HARARE GABORONE
PORTSMOUTH NH (USA)

98 97 96 95 94

10 9 8 7 6 5 4 3 2 1

British Library Cataloguing in Publication Data is available from the British Library on request.

ISBN 0 431 07643 X

Cover designed and pages typeset by Philip Parkhouse
Printed in China

Picture Credits
pp. 2-3, © J. G. Fuller/Hutchison Library; pp. 4-5, © Mark Cator/IMPACT Photos; pp. 6-7, Mark Mille/DeWalt
and Associates, 1991; pp. 8-9, © Steve Kaufman/Bruce Coleman Limited; pp. 10-11, Rick Karpinski/DeWalt
and Associates, 1991; pp. 12-13, © Nicholas De Vore/Bruce Coleman Limited; pp. 14-15,
© Udo Hirsch/Bruce Coleman Limited; pp. 16-17, courtesy of NASA; pp. 18-19, © 1992 Greg Vaughn;
pp. 20-21, © J. G. Fuller/Hutchison Library; pp. 22-23, © Keith Gunnar/Bruce Coleman Limited; p. 24,
© Keith Gunnar/Bruce Coleman Limited

Cover photograph © Tony Stone Worldwide
Back cover photograph © Sygma/D. Kirkland

Series editor: Elizabeth Kaplan
Series designer: Sabine Beaupré
Picture researcher: Diane Laska
Consulting editor: Matthew Groshek

What is the air made up of?

The air surrounding our planet is made up of a mixture of gases. Nitrogen and oxygen are the main gases in the **atmosphere**. **Carbon dioxide** and water vapour are also present in small amounts. We cannot survive without these gases.

carbon dioxide

nitrogen

6

We take in oxygen to release energy from our food. Water vapour falls as rain, giving us water to drink. Plants take in nitrogen, which passes from the air to the soil. Plants use carbon dioxide to make food. In the end, we depend on plants for all our food.

7

oxygen

How does nature pollute the air?

Gases are not the only things floating in our atmosphere. The air naturally contains a certain amount of dirt. Erupting volcanoes spew huge amounts of dust and ash into the air. Natural forest fires and grass fires fill the air with black soot. If a large meteorite hits the Earth, the impact can send tonnes of dirt and rock flying into the atmosphere. The ash, dust, dirt, rock and soot from these natural sources can darken the sky and block sunlight for months or even years.

How do people pollute the air?

Most of the dirt in the air comes from things people do. We throw out enormous piles of rubbish that go up in smoke in huge incinerators. We burn tonnes of coal and oil to generate electricity. We burn natural gas in furnaces for heating. We fill the tanks of our cars with petrol and drive millions of kilometres each year. Our cities and towns are choked with traffic and the air turns into a murky haze.

11

Why are pollutants so unpleasant ?

Burning **fossil fuels** – coal, oil, natural gas and petrol – releases many different pollutants into the air. We can see or smell many of these pollutants. Smoke is black with unburned carbon. Smog is brown with **nitrogen dioxide** and **hydrocarbons**. **Sulphur** gases give off a horrible smell like rotten eggs.

But some of the most dangerous pollutants are invisible. **Carbon monoxide** is released when petrol is burned. This colourless, odourless gas can kill a person in minutes.

Can pollution make you ill?

Dirty air makes many people feel ill. It can make your eyes water. It can make your nose itch. It can make your throat feel dry and sore.

But polluted air does more than simply cause discomfort. Air pollution contributes to many different diseases. People with heart and lung problems find it more difficult to breathe when the air is polluted. They may have to go to hospital if they breathe in too much polluted air. Pollutants in the air even cause some forms of cancer.

Harming the Earth

Air pollution doesn't only harm people. It can affect all life on Earth. Some pollutants, called **chlorofluorocarbons**, or CFCs, are especially dangerous. These chemicals, found in polystyrene containers and refrigerator coolant, actually destroy the part of our atmosphere called the ozone layer. The ozone layer helps protect the Earth from the Sun's burning rays. But CFCs are causing large holes in the ozone layer. In places near these holes, skin cancer is on the increase.

Clean-air campaigns

People have been fighting air pollution for many years. They have persuaded power stations and factories to install **scrubbers** on their chimneys. These devices clean pollutants from smoke. They have made car-makers install **catalytic converters**, which remove some pollutants in car exhausts. They push for more research into forms of energy which cause little air pollution. Wind energy, generated by windmills, shown here, is clean and safe. Solar energy is another clean alternative. Using these forms of energy can reduce levels of pollutants in the air.

What causes the most air pollution?

Of all the things we do, driving cars causes the most air pollution. You can help reduce air pollution by finding other ways to get about instead of by car. You might walk or cycle, instead of accepting a lift. If you do need to go somewhere in a car, try to travel with other people who are going to the same place. Car-sharing helps to cut down on the number of cars on the road, reducing air pollution. Encourage your parents and friends to follow your example in walking, cycling or car-sharing.

21

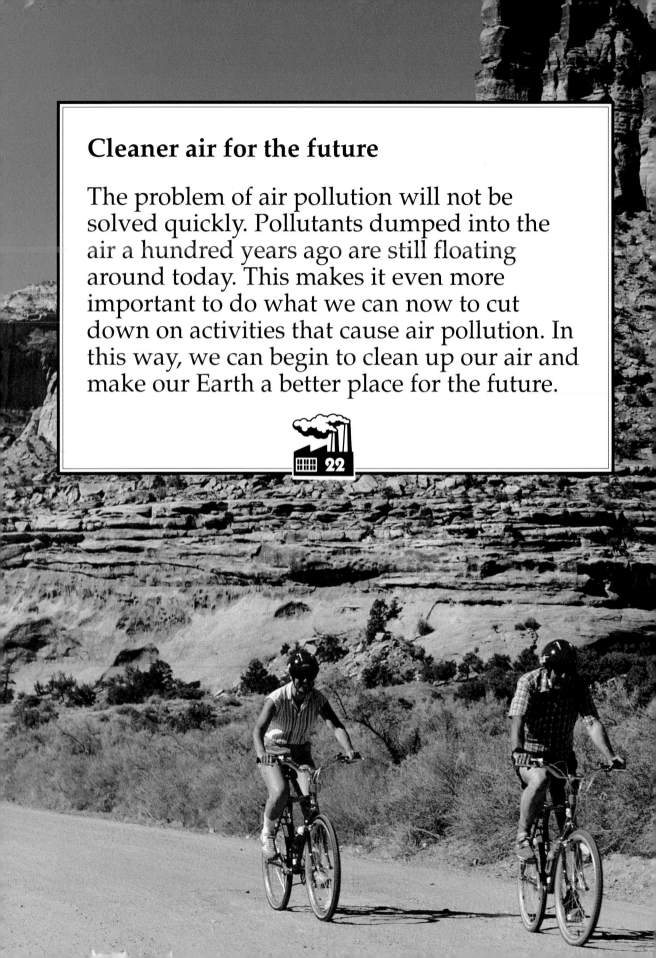

Cleaner air for the future

The problem of air pollution will not be solved quickly. Pollutants dumped into the air a hundred years ago are still floating around today. This makes it even more important to do what we can now to cut down on activities that cause air pollution. In this way, we can begin to clean up our air and make our Earth a better place for the future.

22

Glossary

atmosphere: the gases that surround the Earth

carbon dioxide: a gas in the Earth's atmosphere which contains one atom of carbon and two atoms of oxygen; carbon dioxide traps heat close to the Earth

carbon monoxide: a colourless, odourless gas released when fossil fuels are burned; breathing carbon monoxide can cause death

catalytic converter: a device on a car that helps remove some dangerous gases from car exhausts

chlorofluorocarbon (CFC): a chemical that destroys the ozone layer; CFCs are found in refrigerator and air-conditioning coolant and polystyrene containers

environment: the natural and artificial things that make up our surroundings

fossil fuels: coal, oil, natural gas and petrol; these fuels formed from decaying plant and animal remains buried beneath the Earth's surface millions of years ago

hydrocarbon: a chemical made up of hydrogen and carbon; hydrocarbons combine with other gases in the air to form a yellow or brown haze

nitrogen dioxide: a gas made up of one atom of nitrogen and two atoms of oxygen; it forms a brown haze in the air

scrubbers: devices that clean sulphur and other pollutants out of factory smoke before the smoke is released into the air

sulphur: a chemical element that, in its gaseous state, contributes to

Index